Three Gorges Dam

by Lisa Moran

Table of Contents

Introduction

You have just arrived by boat at a city on a great river. The town is built on a cliff high above the riverbank. You walk up 300 steps from the dock to reach the city gate. The gate is built into the city's old stone wall. A nearby market sells everything from pears to high-heeled shoes.

Near the city gate is a terrace. There are tables and chairs where you can sit and look out over the mighty river below. In the distance is the entrance to a magnificent **gorge**. The cliffs of the river canyon rise steeply into the sky. Boats look small from where you sit.

A ship passes through the Wu Xia Gorge on the Yangtze River.

This is the town of Fengjie (FUNG-jee), China. It is on the banks of the Yangtze (YANK-see) River, the longest river in all of Asia. But Fengjie won't be here much longer. By the year 2009, the entire town will be under water.

Why? China is building the largest **dam** in the world on the Yangtze River. The dam, called the Three Gorges Dam, is creating a manmade lake. When this lake is full, it will completely cover many cities like Fengjie.

China's dam has caused a lot of disagreement. There are people who are in favor of it and people who are against it. The dam will bring some positive changes to China. It will create jobs. It will provide transportation. And it will help control flooding of the Yangtze River. But it will cause many problems, too.

CHAPTER ONE

People and the Dam

The Three Gorges Dam will be the largest dam ever built. It will be more than 600 feet (183 m) tall. It will stretch wider than a mile. The lake it will create is called a **reservoir**. The reservoir will be nearly 400 miles (644 km) long when it is full.

The dam stretches across one of China's Three Gorges. The Three Gorges are made up of steep, rocky cliffs. Villages and ancient **temples** dot the cliffsides.

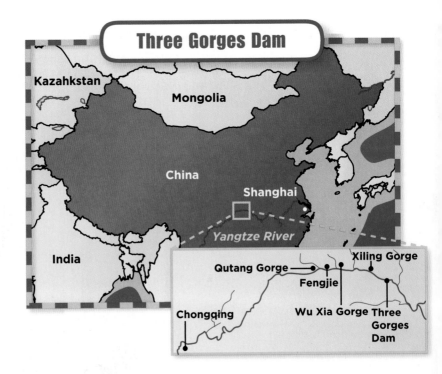

Three Gorges Dam

Kazahkstan

Mongolia

China

Shanghai

Yangtze River

India

Qutang Gorge

Fengjie

Xiling Gorge

Chongqing

Wu Xia Gorge

Three Gorges Dam

Winding through the gorges is the powerful Yangtze River. The Yangtze travels thousands of miles across China. It is the third largest river in the world. The Yangtze has always been very important to those who live near it. Millions of people depend on the river for drinking, farming, and transportation.

China's leaders have long dreamed of using the power of the Yangtze by building a dam across the river. But it was not until 1994 that China started building the Three Gorges Dam.

↻ The reservoir created by the Three Gorges Dam will be so big that it will be visible from outer space.

◠ In the last 100 years, the Yangtze's floods have killed at least 300,000 people.

The government of China believes that the dam will bring many benefits to the country. The building of the dam has already created thousands of jobs. The deep lake will allow large ships to travel farther up the Yangtze than ever before. New business will come to cities that lie inland, far away from the ocean.

The dam will also help control flooding. The Yangtze floods every year, killing many people. The floods also destroy crops and buildings. The new reservoir should absorb, or soak up, some of the floodwaters.

The dam will also provide energy. Water that flows through a dam can make electricity. Electricity made by dams is much cleaner than the energy made by coal-powered plants. Chinese leaders believe that the Three Gorges Dam will produce as much energy as seven coal plants.

But many people do not think that the dam will bring all that it promises. Some argue that the dam is really hurting the people it is supposed to help. The dam's reservoir will cover hundreds of cities and towns. More than one million people have already moved to new homes. Many have left behind places that their families had lived in for generations.

↻ Water flows through huge **turbines**, or motors, like this one. The turbines in the dam will make as much electricity as ten or more nuclear power plants.

The harbor town of Wushan has been knocked down and moved to higher ground to make way for the reservoir.

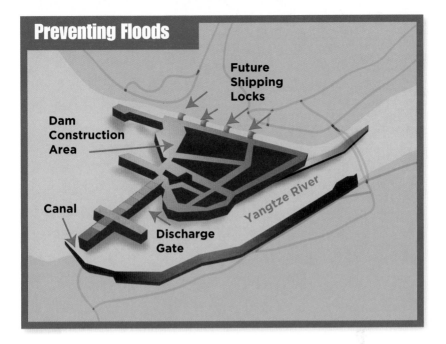

Preventing Floods

Future Shipping Locks

Dam Construction Area

Canal

Discharge Gate

Yangtze River

Others say that the dam will create a problem with **sediment**. Sediment is the dirt that settles at the bottom of a river. It comes from earth that washes off the riverbanks. The Yangtze carries millions of tons of sediment in its waters. Most washes **downstream**. But the dam will prevent the river from flushing its sediment to the sea.

Much of the sediment will back up in the reservoir. This will make the lake shallower. Large ships will not be able to use the lake, and there will be no room for extra water from heavy rains. If the reservoir overflows, millions of people who live downstream could be harmed.

To solve the problem, the dam has special gates. Sediment comes out a discharge gate and flows downstream through a canal.

CHAPTER TWO

History and the Dam

More than a thousand historic sites are located near the area of the dam. They are at risk of being flooded by the new reservoir. Some of the sites are important to the **heritage** of the Chinese people. One site is that of the Ba people.

Not much is known about the Ba. Scientists only found out about them a short time ago. No one completely understands their language or can read their writing. Scholars are still finding objects from the Ba culture.

The city of Fuling was their capital more than 2,000 years ago. The Ba buried their dead in wooden coffins shaped like boats. They placed the coffins into the cliff walls high above the Yangtze.

These royal **tombs** of the Ba are **endangered**. The reservoir could wash them away. Chinese officials say they are doing everything they can to preserve the Ba treasures. But they are in a race against time. Much of this ancient **civilization** could be lost to the rising waters.

⊕ Parts of the city of Fuling will be covered by water when the reservoir fills up.

⌒ A woman in Dachang makes a bamboo basket.

Another important place that may not survive the flooding is the town of Dachang. Dachang lies on a **tributary** of the Yangtze. Its waters flow into the great river. Dachang once had the largest group of houses from the Ming and Qing (CHIN) **Dynasties**. These dynasties ruled China between 1368 and 1912. Many of the old buildings are still standing.

China has saved 37 of Dachang's historical buildings. The government has moved them to a new location 3 miles (5 km) away. Workers have knocked down the rest of the buildings to make way for new structures.

Another special site that is in danger is Dragon Bones Cave. Scientists found fossils of human ancestors in this cave. One jawbone dates back almost two million years. It is the oldest human fossil ever found in Asia.

The Myth of the Three Gorges

The Chinese have a story that tells how the Three Gorges came to be. It is the tale of the great Emperor Yu. He wanted to do something to stop the flooding of the Yangtze River. Yu decided the river should flow through the mountains. Then the cliffs would hold back the floodwaters. With the help of a gigantic ax, Emperor Yu carved out the Three Gorges.

Other historic sites will survive the dam's flood. The Shibaozhai Temple is 12 stories tall. It is just high enough to be rescued. It was built hundreds of years ago, during one of China's dynasties. It is called one of the "eight strange structures of the world."

The Shibaozhai Temple will become an island. The temple is built into the cliff above the Yangtze. Since the town below it will be flooded, the Chinese government is building a special wall around the temple to protect it. The only way to see this unique structure will be from a boat.

The Shibaozhai temple ➲ is made of wood and painted red. It is so big that travelers can see it from the river.

CHAPTER THREE

Nature and the Dam

The city of Chongqing (CHEWNG-ching) sits at the western end of the reservoir. This gives the city something to worry about. The water level of the reservoir is rising. Sediment is piling up in the Yangtze. The dirt may block the city's drains into the river.

Some experts worry that Chongqing is going to overflow with waste. Billions of gallons of **sewage** end up in the Yangtze River every year. The dam is preventing a lot of this waste from washing away. The reservoir could become a liquid dump.

⊙ Sewage flows into the Yangtze River.

Garbage is not the only concern for the river. There are also chemicals. The dam's lake has buried hundreds of factories and coal mines under water. Scientists fear that chemicals from these sites will leak into the river.

⊙ Almost all of the sewage that Chongqing dumps into the river is untreated. That means that no harmful substances have been removed from the waste before it pollutes the water.

◑ Building the dam is an enormous job.

The government of China says it is trying hard to keep the reservoir clean. It is doing a better job of picking up the garbage that people throw into the Yangtze. It is building new plants to clean up sewage before it gets dumped into the river. Chemicals were removed from many factories before they went under water. Trash from garbage dumps was moved to higher ground.

"We will solve these problems," one Chinese official said. Others are not so sure.

Danger to Animals

The Yangtze River is home to many special animals. One of these is the baiji dolphin. Some people consider the baiji a "living fossil." This is because scientists think that the baiji's ancestors were some of the first sea creatures to walk on land.

The baiji is already in danger. There are fewer than 100 of them in the wild. Boat propellers and fishing nets have killed many of them. Dams have cut off lakes that the baiji use for food and raising their young.

The government of China has pledged to help the baiji. It has built a special protected river for the dolphins. But no one is sure how the Three Gorges Dam and the reservoir will affect the baiji.

Siberian White Cranes

Siberian (sigh-BEER-ee-uhn) white cranes are an endangered species. There are not many left in the wild. Siberian cranes fish in a lake that is filled every year when the Yangtze River floods. The Three Gorges Dam will lower the water level in the lake. This might harm the fish and the cranes that feed on them.

The dam will also change the wilderness. Scientists say the air temperature will go up because of the huge reservoir. Some plants may die off in the warmer climate. Some animals will not be able to live in the warm, slow-moving waters of the reservoir. Pollution may kill some animals, too. It's too early to tell how nature will react to the Three Gorges Dam.

↻ Some people have called the well-known baiji dolphins "pandas in the water."

Conclusion

Most of China's leaders are not worried about the dangers of the Three Gorges Dam. They are overjoyed by their ability to build it. But critics say the dam is too costly and risky.

The Three Gorges Dam will not be finished until the year 2009. Until then, the world will wait to see if China has tamed the mighty Yangtze River.

History of Three Gorges Dam

2009
The entire Three Gorges project will be finished.

1994
Construction of the new Three Gorges Dam begins.

2010

2003
The dam is nearly finished. The reservoir begins to fill.

1992
The government of China decides to start building the dam again.

1990

1970

1950

1947
Construction on the dam stops.

1946
The United States begins to help China build the dam.

1930

1919
The leader of China comes up with the idea of a dam in the Three Gorges.

1910

China plans to spend at least $25 billion to build the Three Gorges Dam and reservoir.

Glossary

civilization *(siv-uh-luh-ZAY-shuhn)* a condition of human society in which agriculture, trade, government, art, and science are highly developed *(page 10)*

dam *(DAM)* a wall built to hold back flowing water *(page 3)*

downstream *(DOWN-streem)* moving in the same direction as the current of a stream *(page 9)*

dynasty *(DIGH-nuh-stee)* a time when members of one family ruled a certain place *(page 12)*

endangered *(en-DAYN-juhrd)* threatened with harm or loss *(page 10)*

gorge *(GAWRJ)* a steep, narrow passage between cliffs *(page 2)*

heritage *(HER-i-tij)* something handed down from ancestors or the past, like a way of life *(page 10)*

reservoir *(REZ-uhr-vwahr)* a place where water is collected and stored *(page 4)*

sediment *(SED-uh-muhnt)* matter, like dirt, that settles at the bottom of water *(page 9)*

sewage *(SEW-ij)* waste carried off by drains *(page 15)*

temple *(TEM-puhl)* a building used for worship *(page 4)*

tomb *(TEWM)* a grave or building in which a dead body is placed *(page 10)*

tributary *(TRIB-yuh-te-ree)* a river or stream that flows into a larger river *(page 12)*

turbine *(TUR-bighn)* a motor *(page 7)*

Index

Comprehension Check

Summarize

Write a brief paragraph that summarizes the facts and opinions about the Three Gorges Dam.

Think and Compare

1. Reread pages 15 through 17. What are some facts about what the Three Gorges Dam will do to the river and its natural surroundings? What are some opinions? How can you tell the difference between the opinions and the facts?
   (Evaluate Fact and Opinion)

2. What do you think of China's idea to build the Three Gorges dam? Do you think it will be good for the Chinese people? Or do you believe that it will cause more problems? Give facts from the story to support your opinion. **(Analyze)**

3. Why do you think other countries should pay attention to what happens with the Three Gorges Dam? Why might China's dam be important to the rest of the world? **(Evaluate)**